GW00630742

MEMORIES OF STEAM
DESK DIARY 2012

D&C
David and Charles

Ex-GWR 'Castle' Class 4-6-0 No. 5042 'Winchester Castle' makes a fine sight as it heads the 'Merchant Venturer' express at Milepost 105¾ on the eastern outskirts of Bath on 30 April 1960. Built in 1935, this locomotive spent most of its BR days located to Gloucester Horton Road depot until withdrawal in June 1965.

DECEMBER /JANUARY

Boxing Day

26
Monday

Bank Holiday

27
Tuesday

28
Wednesday

29
Thursday

30
Friday

31
Saturday

New Year's Day

1
Sunday

DECEMBER						
M	T	W	T	F	S	S
			1	2	3	4
5	6	7	8	9	10	11
12	13	14	15	16	17	18
19	20	21	22	23	24	25
26	27	28	29	30	31	

Two ex-LMS 'Jubilee' Class 4-6-0s alongside Threlfall's Brewer in Manchester in the early 1960s. On the left No. 45650 'Blake' runs towards Victoria station with a train from Blackpool while on the right No. 45661 'Vernon' heads out of town with the morning express to Glasgow and Edinburgh. 'Blake' was withdrawn in January 1963 while 'Vernon' survived until May 1965.

JANUARY

Bank Holiday (UK)

2
Monday

3
Tuesday

4
Wednesday

5
Thursday

6
Friday

7
Saturday

8
Sunday

			JANUARY			
M	T	W	T	F	S	S
						1
2	3	4	5	6	7	8
9	10	11	12	13	14	15
16	17	18	19	20	21	22
23	24	25	26	27	28	29
30	31					

Ex-GWR 'Grange' Class 4-6-0 No. 6874 'Haughton Grange' departs from Plymouth with
the overnight Paddington to Penzance train on the morning of 7 September 1962. The loco spent
its last days working out of Oxford depot until withdrawal in September 1965. No members of this
class were preserved but brand new No. 6880 'Betton Grange' is currently being built at Llangollen
Railway Works using some parts from 'Hall' Class 4-6-0 No. 5952 'Cogan Hall'.

JANUARY

9
Monday

10
Tuesday

11
Wednesday

12
Thursday

13
Friday

14
Saturday

15
Sunday

			JANUARY			
M	T	W	T	F	S	S
						1
2	3	4	5	6	7	8
9	10	11	12	13	14	15
16	17	18	19	20	21	22
23	24	25	26	27	28	29
30	31					

BR Standard Class 7MT 'Britannia' Class 4-6-2 No. 70016 'Ariel' of Plymouth Laira depot heads along the sea wall at Teignmouth with a down express on 26 July 1955. Some members of this class were delivered new to Old Oak Common and Laira depots but were soon transferred to Cardiff Canton from where they put in good performances on South Wales expresses to Paddington. Like the rest of its class No. 70016 spent its last years working on the West Coast Main Line north of Crewe until withdrawal in August 1967.

JANUARY

16
Monday

17
Tuesday

18
Wednesday

19
Thursday

20
Friday

21
Saturday

22
Sunday

JANUARY						
M	T	W	T	F	S	S
						1
2	3	4	5	6	7	8
9	10	11	12	13	14	15
16	17	18	19	20	21	22
23	24	25	26	27	28	29
30	31					

Carrying the superstitious '666' train reporting number and fitted with a straight-sided Hawksworth tender, BR-built 'Castle' Class 4-6-0 No. 7015 'Carn Brea Castle' is seen hard at work on the 1 in 42 Hemerdon Bank east of Plymouth with a northbound train composed entirely of ex-LNER stock on 6 August 1956. Built at Swindon in 1948 and subsequently fitted with a double chimney and four-row superheater, this fine loco had a short working life before withdrawal in April 1963.

JANUARY

Chinese New Year

23
Monday

24
Tuesday

25
Wednesday

26
Thursday

27
Friday

28
Saturday

29
Sunday

JANUARY						
M	T	W	T	F	S	S
						1
2	3	4	5	6	7	8
9	10	11	12	13	14	15
16	17	18	19	20	21	22
23	24	25	26	27	28	29
30	31					

BR-built 'Castle' Class 4-6-0 No. 7005 'Sir Edward Elgar' heads the 1.15pm express from Paddington to Hereford near Maidenhead on a wintry 28 December 1962. Originally named 'Lamphey Castle' this loco was renamed in 1957 after the famous Worcestershire composer and spent most of its life working out of Worcester depot until withdrawal in September 1964.

JANUARY/FEBRUARY

30
Monday

31
Tuesday

1
Wednesday

2
Thursday

3
Friday

4
Saturday

5
Sunday

FEBRUARY						
M	T	W	T	F	S	S
		1	2	3	4	5
6	7	8	9	10	11	12
13	14	15	16	17	18	19
20	21	22	23	24	25	26
27	28	29				

Ex-GWR 'County' Class 4-6-0 No. 1027 'County of Stafford' of Swindon depot climbs out of Mill Lane Tunnel, Box, with an eastbound goods train on 16 April 1963. This loco was withdrawn six months later and no members of this class were preserved. However, a new-build No. 1014 'County of Glamorgan' is currently being constructed by the Great Western Society at Didcot.

FEBRUARY

6
Monday

7
Tuesday

8
Wednesday

9
Thursday

10
Friday

11
Saturday

12
Sunday

FEBRUARY

M	T	W	T	F	S	S
		1	2	3	4	5
6	7	8	9	10	11	12
13	14	15	16	17	18	19
20	21	22	23	24	25	26
27	28	29				

Ex-LNER 'A4' 4-6-2 No. 60010 'Dominion of Canada' storms out of Gas Works Tunnel with the 10.25am King's Cross to Peterborough train on 27 April 1963. Withdrawn in May 1965, this loco subsequently crossed the Atlantic and is currently a static exhibit at the Canadian Railway Museum. Along with fellow classmate No. 60008 'Dwight D. Eisenhower', which is on display at the National Railroad Museum in Wisconsin, it would make every 'streak'-lovers dream come true if this engine was repatriated to the UK.

FEBRUARY

13
Monday

Valentine's Day

14
Tuesday

15
Wednesday

16
Thursday

17
Friday

18
Saturday

19
Sunday

FEBRUARY

M	T	W	T	F	S	S
		1	2	3	4	5
6	7	8	9	10	11	12
13	14	15	16	17	18	19
20	21	22	23	24	25	26
27	28	29				

With only six weeks to go before the closure of King's Cross depot, Peppercorn Class 'A1' 4-6-2 nears the end of its journey to London while hauling a special train for the Schoolboys International Match past Belle Isle signalbox on 27 April 1963. On the left 'A4' Class 4-6-2 No. 60010 'Dominion of Canada' backs down to King's Cross before hauling the 10.25am train to Peterborough. Steam lovers please try and ignore the Brush Type 2 diesel lurking behind!

FEBRUARY

20
Monday

Shrove Tuesday

21
Tuesday

22
Wednesday

23
Thursday

24
Friday

25
Saturday

26
Sunday

FEBRUARY						
M	T	W	T	F	S	S
		1	2	3	4	5
6	7	8	9	10	11	12
13	14	15	16	17	18	19
20	21	22	23	24	25	26
27	28	29				

Minus its valuable 'Bon Accord' nameplates and with only three months to go before withdrawal, BR-built Peppercorn 'A1' Class 4-6-2 No. 60154 departs from York with the 8.45am Leeds to Glasgow train on 10 July 1965. This loco was one of five of its class to be fitted with Timken roller bearings. This extended the period between their heavy overhauls. Although none of this class of loco was preserved, new-build No. 60163 'Tornado' has been an enormous hit with the public since it arrived on the main line steam scene in 2009.

FEBRUARY/MARCH

27
Monday

28
Tuesday

29
Wednesday

1
Thursday

2
Friday

3
Saturday

4
Sunday

MARCH						
M	T	W	T	F	S	S
			1	2	3	4
5	6	7	8	9	10	11
12	13	14	15	16	17	18
19	20	21	22	23	24	25
26	27	28	29	30	31	

Fitted with German-style smoke deflectors, ex-LNER Class 'A3' No. 60092 'Fairway' hisses down from Heaton depot and through the centre road at Newcastle Central station before taking over a southbound train in 1960. Named after the winner of the 1928 St Leger, this loco was built at Doncaster in the same year and withdrawn in October 1964. Fortunately its famous classmate, No. 60103 'Flying Scotsman' will soon be seen in steam again after a major overhaul at the National Railway Museum, York.

MARCH

5
Monday

6
Tuesday

7
Wednesday

8
Thursday

9
Friday

10
Saturday

11
Sunday

MARCH						
M	T	W	T	F	S	S
			1	2	3	4
5	6	7	8	9	10	11
12	13	14	15	16	17	18
19	20	21	22	23	24	25
26	27	28	29	30	31	

Ex-LNER Class 'A4' No. 60034 'Lord Faringdon' moves off from Newcastle Central with the 10am express to King's Cross on a winter's morning in 1957. Originally named 'Peregrine' this loco was built at Doncaster in 1938 and spent its last years operating out of Aberdeen Ferryhill depot hauling the 3-hour Glasgow to Aberdeen expresses until withdrawal in August 1966.

MARCH

12 Monday

13 Tuesday

14 Wednesday

15 Thursday

16 Friday

St Patrick's Day

17 Saturday

Mother's Day (UK)

18 Sunday

MARCH						
M	T	W	T	F	S	S
			1	2	3	4
5	6	7	8	9	10	11
12	13	14	15	16	17	18
19	20	21	22	23	24	25
26	27	28	29	30	31	

Ex-LMS 'Royal Scot' Class 4-6-0 No. 46115 of Carlisle Kingmoor shed heads south near Carstairs with a parcels train on 16 April 1965. By then devoid of its nameplates, 'Scots Guardsman' had had an illustrious career starring in the famous 1936 GPO Film Unit documentary *Night Mail* which featured a poem by W H Auden and music by Benjamin Britten. In January 1966 the loco became the last of its class to be withdrawn but was fortunately saved for preservation and returned to main line running in 2008.

MARCH

19
Monday

20
Tuesday

21
Wednesday

22
Thursday

23
Friday

24
Saturday

25
Sunday

		MARCH				
M	T	W	T	F	S	S
				1	2	3	4
5	6	7	8	9	10	11
12	13	14	15	16	17	18
19	20	21	22	23	24	25
26	27	28	29	30	31	

In ex-works condition, ex-GWR 'Hall' Class 4-6-0 No. 6952 'Kimberley Hall' heads an inter-regional train from Bournemouth to Wolverhampton Low Level at Basingstoke station on 22 August 1964. Built at Swindon in 1943, this loco was withdrawn from Tyseley shed at the end of 1965.

MARCH/APRIL

26
Monday

27
Tuesday

28
Wednesday

29
Thursday

30
Friday

31
Saturday

1
Sunday

MARCH						
M	T	W	T	F	S	S
			1	2	3	4
5	6	7	8	9	10	11
12	13	14	15	16	17	18
19	20	21	22	23	24	25
26	27	28	29	30	31	

Ex-GWR 0-6-0PTs Nos. 4610 and 4694 give rear end assistance to a bulk cement train at Exeter St David's station on 1 September 1964. The heavy train, double-headed by Ivatt Class 2 2-6-2T No. 41295 and 'Hall' Class 4-6-0 No. 6925 'Hackness Hall' was about to tackle the 1 in 37 incline to Central station. Diesel traction soon replaced this once familiar scene at Exeter.

APRIL

2
Monday

3
Tuesday

4
Wednesday

5
Thursday

Good Friday

6
Friday

7
Saturday

Easter Sunday

8
Sunday

			APRIL			
M	T	W	T	F	S	S
						1
2	3	4	5	6	7	8
9	10	11	12	13	14	15
16	17	18	19	20	21	22
23	24	25	26	27	28	29
30						

Ex-LMS 'Jubilee' Class 4-6-0 No. 45565 'Victoria' makes a spirited start out of Gloucester Eastgate and across Barton Street level crossing with an express for Bristol on 1 January 1965. This scene was soon to disappear with steam eradicated from Gloucester at the end of the year and the former Midland Railway mainline from Eastgate to Tuffley Junction closing completely at the end of 1975. Built by the North British Locomotive Company in 1934, 'Victoria' survived until January 1967 when it was withdrawn.

APRIL

Easter Monday

9
Monday

10
Tuesday

11
Wednesday

12
Thursday

13
Friday

14
Saturday

15
Sunday

APRIL						
M	T	W	T	F	S	S
						1
2	3	4	5	6	7	8
9	10	11	12	13	14	15
16	17	18	19	20	21	22
23	24	25	26	27	28	29
30						

BR-built 'Castle' Class 4-6-0 No. 7005 'Sir Edward Elgar' waits to take over an LCGB special train to London at Cheltenham Lansdown on 12 October 1963. The special had arrived at Cheltenham behind ex-LMS 'Jubilee' Class 4-6-0 No. 45552 'Silver Jubilee'.

APRIL

16
Monday

17
Tuesday

18
Wednesday

19
Thursday

20
Friday

21
Saturday

22
Sunday

APRIL

M	T	W	T	F	S	S
						1
2	3	4	5	6	7	8
9	10	11	12	13	14	15
16	17	18	19	20	21	22
23	24	25	26	27	28	29
30						

A Sunday afternoon line-up at the rear of Gloucester Barnwood depot on 15 September 1963. From right to left: BR Standard Class 4MT 4-6-0 No. 75061; Ex-LMS Stanier 8F 2-8-0 No. 48095; BR Standard 9F 2-10-0s Nos 92082 and 92111; ex-LMS Fowler 4F 0-6-0 No. 43979; ex-LMS Stanier 8F 2-8-0 No. 48179. Barnwood depot closed in May 1964.

APRIL

23
Monday

24
Tuesday

25
Wednesday

26
Thursday

27
Friday

28
Saturday

29
Sunday

			APRIL			
M	T	W	T	F	S	S
						1
2	3	4	5	6	7	8
9	10	11	12	13	14	15
16	17	18	19	20	21	22
23	24	25	26	27	28	29
30						

BR Standard Class 9F 2-10-0 No. 92123 takes on water in the wintry sunshine at Gloucester Horton Road depot on 1 January 1965. A year later this scene was to disappear forever when Horton Road shed closed to steam. Nine of these powerful locos were saved for preservation.

APRIL/MAY

30
Monday

1
Tuesday

2
Wednesday

3
Thursday

4
Friday

5
Saturday

6
Sunday

			MAY			
M	T	W	T	F	S	S
	1	2	3	4	5	6
7	8	9	10	11	12	13
14	15	16	17	18	19	20
21	22	23	24	25	26	27
28	29	30	31			

A GWR steam lineup at Newton Abbot depot on 18 May 1958. From left to right: 'Castle' Class 4-6-0 No. 4089 'Donnington Castle' (behind is No. 5195 and No. 7000); 2-6-2T No. 5108; 'Modified Hall' Class 4-6-0 No. 6988 'Swithland Hall' (No. 5553 behind); 2-6-2Ts No. 5154 and 4145. The depot closed to steam on 1 April 1962 whereas the nearby publishers, David & Charles, continue to publish fine railway books!

MAY

Bank Holiday (UK)

7
Monday

8
Tuesday

9
Wednesday

10
Thursday

11
Friday

12
Saturday

13
Sunday

MAY						
M	T	W	T	F	S	S
	1	2	3	4	5	6
7	8	9	10	11	12	13
14	15	16	17	18	19	20
21	22	23	24	25	26	27
28	29	30	31			

Rebuilt 'Battle of Britain' Class 4-6-2 No. 34071 '601 Squadron' waits to depart from Salisbury with a West of England express in 1962. This Bulleid-designed loco was the first of its class to be built by British Railways when it emerged from Brighton Works in April 1948.
It was rebuilt in 1960 and withdrawn in 1967.

MAY

14
Monday

15
Tuesday

16
Wednesday

17
Thursday

18
Friday

19
Saturday

20
Sunday

			MAY			
M	T	W	T	F	S	S
	1	2	3	4	5	6
7	8	9	10	11	12	13
14	15	16	17	18	19	20
21	22	23	24	25	26	27
28	29	30	31			

Fitted with German-style smoke deflectors, ex-LNER Class 'A3' 4-6-2 No. 60109 'Hermit' of King's Cross depot departs from Leeds Central with an express for King's Cross in the late 1950s. Originally built as an 'A1' in 1923 this loco was rebuilt as an 'A3' in 1943 and withdrawn in November 1962. Behind is Peppercorn Class 'A1' 4-6-2 No. 60123 'H. A. Ivatt' which became the first of its class to be withdrawn after an accident at Offord on the East Coast Main Line in 1962.

MAY

21
Monday

22
Tuesday

23
Wednesday

24
Thursday

25
Friday

26
Saturday

27
Sunday

			MAY			
M	T	W	T	F	S	S
	1	2	3	4	5	6
7	8	9	10	11	12	13
14	15	16	17	18	19	20
21	22	23	24	25	26	27
28	29	30	31			

Sporting an Aberdeen Ferryhill shed plate, ex-LNER Class 'A4' 4-6-2 No. 60024 'Kingfisher' backs out of Glasgow's Buchanan Street station after hauling a three-hour express from Aberdeen on 23 August 1966. Along with fellow class member No. 60019 'Bittern' this loco was the last member of its class to remain in service until withdrawal two weeks later — 'Bittern' was saved for preservation but, sadly, 'Kingfisher' ended up on the scrap heap.

MAY/JUNE

28
Monday

29
Tuesday

30
Wednesday

31
Thursday

1
Friday

2
Saturday

3
Sunday

JUNE						
M	T	W	T	F	S	S
				1	2	3
4	5	6	7	8	9	10
11	12	13	14	15	16	17
18	19	20	21	22	23	24
25	26	27	28	29	30	

Allocated to Manchester Longsight depot, ex-LMS unrebuilt 'Patriot' Class 4-6-0 No. 45501 'St Dunstans' rolls into Stockport with a train for the West of England on 18 November 1953. Along with fellow class member No. 45500 'Patriot' this loco was a 1930 rebuild (at Derby Works) of an LNWR 'Claughton' Class 4-6-0 and was withdrawn in September 1961. The class were known as 'Baby Scots' due to their similarity to the 'Royal Scot' Class of locos.

JUNE

Spring Bank Holiday (UK)

4
Monday

5
Tuesday

6
Wednesday

7
Thursday

8
Friday

9
Saturday

10
Sunday

JUNE						
M	T	W	T	F	S	S
				1	2	3
4	5	6	7	8	9	10
11	12	13	14	15	16	17
18	19	20	21	22	23	24
25	26	27	28	29	30	

Originally allocated to Cardiff Canton depot, BR Standard 'Britannia' Class 4-6-2 No. 70022 (minus its 'Tornado' nameplates) climbs the 1 in 75 gradient to Shap Summit past Scout Green signal cabin with an early morning northbound parcels train on 1 June 1966. The train is assisted in the rear by Tebay banker Class 4 2-6-4 tank No. 42225. Poor old 'Tornado' was dispatched to the breaker's yard at the end of 1967 but the name has since been revived on the new-build Class 'A1' 4-6-2 No. 60163.

JUNE

11 Monday

12 Tuesday

13 Wednesday

14 Thursday

15 Friday

16 Saturday

Father's Day (US/UK)

17 Sunday

			JUNE			
M	T	W	T	F	S	S
				1	2	3
4	5	6	7	8	9	10
11	12	13	14	15	16	17
18	19	20	21	22	23	24
25	26	27	28	29	30	

Ex-LMS unrebuilt 'Patriot' Class 4-6-0 No. 45524 'Blackpool' tackles the 1 in 112 gradient near Linthwaite, Huddersfield, Yorkshire, while hauling a Hull to Liverpool express in the late 1950s. This loco was built at Crewe in 1933 and was originally named 'Sir Frederick Harrison' until being renamed in 1937. It was withdrawn in September 1962.

JUNE

18
Monday

19
Tuesday

20
Wednesday

21
Thursday

22
Friday

23
Saturday

24
Sunday

JUNE						
M	T	W	T	F	S	S
				1	2	3
4	5	6	7	8	9	10
11	12	13	14	15	16	17
18	19	20	21	22	23	24
25	26	27	28	29	30	

Devoid of its 'The King's Royal Rifle Corps' nameplates, ex-LMS 'Royal Scot' Class 4-6-0 No. 46140 arrives at Carlisle with the 9am Perth to Euston express on 18 April 1965. The loco was originally built with a parallel boiler and named 'Hector' in 1927, rebuilt with a Stanier taper boiler in 1952 and withdrawn in November 1965.

JUNE/JULY

25
Monday

26
Tuesday

27
Wednesday

28
Thursday

29
Friday

30
Saturday

1
Sunday

JUNE						
M	T	W	T	F	S	S
				1	2	3
4	5	6	7	8	9	10
11	12	13	14	15	16	17
18	19	20	21	22	23	24
25	26	27	28	29	30	

One of the few unnamed members of its class, ex-LMS unrebuilt 'Patriot' Class 4-6-0 No. 45517 makes a splendid sight while hard at work in the Cumbrian Fells on the approach to Shap. This loco was built at Crewe in 1933 and withdrawn in June 1962. Despite no members of this class being preserved a new-build loco, No. 45551 'The Unknown Warrior', is currently under construction at the Llangollen Railway Works.

JULY

2
Monday

3
Tuesday

Independence Day (US)

4
Wednesday

5
Thursday

6
Friday

7
Saturday

8
Sunday

JULY						
M	T	W	T	F	S	S
						1
2	3	4	5	6	7	8
9	10	11	12	13	14	15
16	17	18	19	20	21	22
23	24	25	26	27	28	29
30	31					

Ex-GWR '4500' Class 2-6-2T No. 4507 is seen at the head of a local train for Yeovil Town at Taunton in August 1960. When new in 1907 this was the last locomotive to be built at Wolverhampton Works from which date all GWR loco building was concentrated at Swindon. This historic and long-lived loco was withdrawn from Yeovil Town shed in October 1963.

JULY

9
Monday

10
Tuesday

11
Wednesday

12
Thursday

13
Friday

14
Saturday

15
Sunday

		JULY				
M	T	W	T	F	S	S
						1
2	3	4	5	6	7	8
9	10	11	12	13	14	15
16	17	18	19	20	21	22
23	24	25	26	27	28	29
30	31					

Deputising for a failed 'Castle', ex-GWR 'Modified Hall' 4-6-0 No. 6999 'Capel Dewi Hall' speeds through Bruton, Somerset, while hauling a non-stop Paddington to Plymouth Ian Allan excursion on 9 May 1964. The train was organised to commemorate the 60th anniversary of the record-breaking run of 4-4-0 'City of Truro' when it became the first steam locomotive in the world to (supposedly) reach 100mph (down Wellington Bank with the wind behind it). Even the correct headboard on No. 6999 seems to have gone astray!

JULY

16
Monday

17
Tuesday

18
Wednesday

19
Thursday

20
Friday

21
Saturday

22
Sunday

			JULY			
M	T	W	T	F	S	S
						1
2	3	4	5	6	7	8
9	10	11	12	13	14	15
16	17	18	19	20	21	22
23	24	25	26	27	28	29
30	31					

Dwarfed by the new Tamar road bridge, 'County' Class 4-6-0 No. 1006 'County of Cornwall' enters Saltash after crossing Brunel's famous Saltash Bridge with the 3.46pm Plymouth to Penzance stopping train on 7 September 1962. No. 1006 was built at Swindon in 1945 and spent most of its life in Cornwall. It was withdrawn from Swindon depot in September 1963.

JULY

23
Monday

24
Tuesday

25
Wednesday

26
Thursday

27
Friday

28
Saturday

29
Sunday

		JULY				
M	T	W	T	F	S	S
						1
2	3	4	5	6	7	8
9	10	11	12	13	14	15
16	17	18	19	20	21	22
23	24	25	26	27	28	29
30	31					

Unrebuilt 'Battle of Britain' Class 4-6-2 No. 34079 '141 Squadron' passes through Plymouth North Road station with a milk train in the early 1960s. Then allocated to Exmouth Junction depot, No. 34079 was built by BR at Brighton in 1948 and withdrawn from service in early 1966.

JULY/AUGUST

30 Monday

31 Tuesday

1 Wednesday

2 Thursday

3 Friday

4 Saturday

5 Sunday

AUGUST						
M	T	W	T	F	S	S
		1	2	3	4	5
6	7	8	9	10	11	12
13	14	15	16	17	18	19
20	21	22	23	24	25	26
27	28	29	30	31		

Watching the trains go by — a lone trainspotter watches as ex-works unrebuilt 'Patriot' Class 4-6-0 No. 45503 'The Royal Leicestershire Regiment' restarts a long mixed goods train near Hartford station, south of Weaver Junction on 17 February 1952. Built at Crewe in 1932 the 'Pat' was withdrawn from Carlisle Upperby depot in August 1961.

AUGUST

6
Monday

7
Tuesday

8
Wednesday

9
Thursday

10
Friday

11
Saturday

12
Sunday

			AUGUST			
M	T	W	T	F	S	S
		1	2	3	4	5
6	7	8	9	10	11	12
13	14	15	16	17	18	19
20	21	22	23	24	25	26
27	28	29	30	31		

Raw Stanier power up Shap — then allocated to Carlisle Upperby depot, ex-LMS 'Coronation' Class 4-6-2 No. 46225 'Duchess of Gloucester' makes a fine sight as she powers up Shap in the early 1960s. The 'Duchess' was built at Crewe with a streamlined casing in 1938, de-streamlined in 1947 and withdrawn in October 1964.

AUGUST

13
Monday

14
Tuesday

15
Wednesday

16
Thursday

17
Friday

18
Saturday

19
Sunday

AUGUST						
M	T	W	T	F	S	S
			1	2	3	4	5
6	7	8	9	10	11	12
13	14	15	16	17	18	19
20	21	22	23	24	25	26
27	28	29	30	31		

Ex-LNER Class 'A3' 4-6-2 No. 60035 'Windsor Lad' looks immaculate in this photo taken at Edinburgh Haymarket depot in the late 1950s. Built at Doncaster in 1934 and named after the winner of the 1934 Derby and St Leger, No. 60035 spent most of its life based in Edinburgh until being withdrawn in September 1961 and cut up at its birthplace one month later.

AUGUST

20
Monday

21
Tuesday

22
Wednesday

23
Thursday

24
Friday

25
Saturday

26
Sunday

AUGUST						
M	T	W	T	F	S	S
		1	2	3	4	5
6	7	8	9	10	11	12
13	14	15	16	17	18	19
20	21	22	23	24	25	26
27	28	29	30	31		

A classic scene of Gresley Pacifics at King's Cross in 1962 — 'A3' Class No. 60109 'Hermit' (fitted with German-style smoke deflectors) and record-breaking 'A4' No. 60022 'Mallard' have just arrived with trains from the north. Both allocated to King's Cross depot, No. 60109 was built in 1923 as an LNER 'A1' Class, rebuilt as an 'A3' in 1943 and withdrawn in November 1962. No. 60022, holder of the world record for steam locos of 126mph, was built in 1938 and withdrawn in April 1963. It has since been preserved at can be see at the National Railway Museum 'Locomotion' at Shildon.

AUGUST/SEPTEMBER

Summer Bank Holiday (UK)

27
Monday

28
Tuesday

29
Wednesday

30
Thursday

31
Friday

1
Saturday

2
Sunday

AUGUST						
M	T	W	T	F	S	S
		1	2	3	4	5
6	7	8	9	10	11	12
13	14	15	16	17	18	19
20	21	22	23	24	25	26
27	28	29	30	31		

The arrival of the up and down 'Atlantic Coast Express' always heralded a short but busy time at Salisbury station each day. Here, 'Merchant Navy' Class 4-6-2 No. 35013 'Blue Funnel' is serviced as it heads the up 'ACE' on 18 April 1964. Built at Eastleigh in 1945. No. 35013 was rebuilt in 1956 and withdrawn in July 1967. The last 'ACE' ran at the end of the summer timetable in September 1964.

SEPTEMBER

3
Monday

4
Tuesday

5
Wednesday

6
Thursday

7
Friday

8
Saturday

9
Sunday

SEPTEMBER						
M	T	W	T	F	S	S
					1	2
3	4	5	6	7	8	9
10	11	12	13	14	15	16
17	18	19	20	21	22	23
24	25	26	27	28	29	30

Fitted with double chimney and four-row superheater, BR-built 'Castle' Class 4-6-0 No. 7018 'Drysllwyn Castle' of Bristol Bath Road depot prepares to leave Bristol Temple Meads station with the up non-stop 'Bristolian' to Paddington in the late 1950s. Occasionally completing the up journey via Badminton in under 94 minutes, the highly successful 'Castles' were replaced by 'Warship' diesel hydraulics in 1959.

SEPTEMBER

10
Monday

11
Tuesday

12
Wednesday

13
Thursday

14
Friday

15
Saturday

16
Sunday

SEPTEMBER						
M	T	W	T	F	S	S
					1	2
3	4	5	6	7	8	9
10	11	12	13	14	15	16
17	18	19	20	21	22	23
24	25	26	27	28	29	30

Rebuilt 'West Country' Class 4-6-2 No. 34013 'Okehampton' is seen at Brighton terminus with a train from Southampton in the late 1950s. Third-rail electrification had come early to Brighton with steam being ousted on the main line to London Victoria as early as 1933. No. 34013 was built at Brighton Works in 1945, rebuilt in 1957 and withdrawn in July 1967.

SEPTEMBER

17
Monday

18
Tuesday

19
Wednesday

20
Thursday

21
Friday

22
Saturday

23
Sunday

SEPTEMBER						
M	T	W	T	F	S	S
					1	2
3	4	5	6	7	8	9
10	11	12	13	14	15	16
17	18	19	20	21	22	23
24	25	26	27	28	29	30

Fitted with an eight-wheel tender, ex-SR Class 'S15' 4-6-0 No. 30829 arrives at Exeter Central with a train of empty ballast wagons en route to Meldon Quarry on 1 August 1962. One of ten such locos then allocated to Salisbury depot these powerful goods locos were also employed on stopping passenger services. Although all had been withdrawn by 1966 seven have since been preserved.

SEPTEMBER

24
Monday

25
Tuesday

26
Wednesday

27
Thursday

28
Friday

29
Saturday

30
Sunday

SEPTEMBER						
M	T	W	T	F	S	S
					1	2
3	4	5	6	7	8	9
10	11	12	13	14	15	16
17	18	19	20	21	22	23
24	25	26	27	28	29	30

On occasions when ECML trains were diverted from Ferryhill to Northallerton via Stockton-on-Tees it was usual for the Darlington standby Pacific to be kept at Eaglescliffe or Bowesfield. Here, Peppercorn Class 'A1' 4-6-2 No. 60124 (minus its 'Kenilworth' nameplates) leaves Eaglescliffe on 26 September 1965. The loco was built at Doncaster in 1949 and withdrawn in March 1966.

OCTOBER

1
Monday

2
Tuesday

3
Wednesday

4
Thursday

5
Friday

6
Saturday

7
Sunday

		OCTOBER				
M	T	W	T	F	S	S
1	2	3	4	5	6	7
8	9	10	11	12	13	14
15	16	17	18	19	20	21
22	23	24	25	26	27	28
29	30	31				

Ex-LNER Class 'D49/2' 4-4-0 No. 62739 'The Badsworth' of Scarborough depot leaves the seaside town with an express for Hull in the late 1950s. Named after mainly north eastern shires and hunts the D49/2 locos were fitted with Lenz Rotary Cam poppet valves. No. 62739 was built in 1932 and withdrawn in October 1960.

OCTOBER

Columbus Day (US)

8
Monday

9
Tuesday

10
Wednesday

11
Thursday

12
Friday

13
Saturday

14
Sunday

OCTOBER

M	T	W	T	F	S	S
1	2	3	4	5	6	7
8	9	10	11	12	13	14
15	16	17	18	19	20	21
22	23	24	25	26	27	28
29	30	31				

Allocated to Camden depot, ex-LMS 'Royal Scot' Class 4-6-0 No. 46118 'Royal Welch Fusilier' waits to depart from Crewe with the 7.45am Sunday-only Blackpool to Euston express in May 1950. The loco was built originally with a parallel boiler in 1927, rebuilt with a Stanier taper boiler in 1946 and withdrawn in June 1964.

OCTOBER

15
Monday

16
Tuesday

17
Wednesday

18
Thursday

19
Friday

20
Saturday

21
Sunday

OCTOBER						
M	T	W	T	F	S	S
1	2	3	4	5	6	7
8	9	10	11	12	13	14
15	16	17	18	19	20	21
22	23	24	25	26	27	28
29	30	31				

In the final year of operation of this famous train, ex-LNER 'A4' No. 60014 'Silver Link' leaves Edinburgh Waverley with the up non-stop 'Elizabethan' express to King's Cross on 20 August 1961. The first of this illustrious class to be built, No. 60014 emerged from Doncaster Works in 1935 and was withdrawn from King's Cross depot at the end of 1962. Some 'A4s' were fitted with corridor tenders to enable a crew-change on this non-stop service.

OCTOBER

22
Monday

23
Tuesday

24
Wednesday

25
Thursday

26
Friday

27
Saturday

28
Sunday

OCTOBER						
M	T	W	T	F	S	S
1	2	3	4	5	6	7
8	9	10	11	12	13	14
15	16	17	18	19	20	21
22	23	24	25	26	27	28
29	30	31				

The final year of steam at Crewe South shed — BR Standard 'Britannia' Class 7MT 4-6-2 No. 70052 (minus its 'Firth of Tay' nameplates) awaits its next turn of duty on 1 March 1967. The loco was one of the final batch of 'Britannias' built at Crewe in 1954 and was withdrawn in April 1967. Crewe South depot closed in November of that year.

OCTOBER/NOVEMBER

29
Monday

30
Tuesday

Halloween

31
Wednesday

1
Thursday

2
Friday

3
Saturday

4
Sunday

NOVEMBER						
M	T	W	T	F	S	S
			1	2	3	4
5	6	7	8	9	10	11
12	13	14	15	16	17	18
19	20	21	22	23	24	25
26	27	28	29	30		

The final standard gauge steam train on BR was run on 11 August, 1968. Here, the 'Six Guinea Special' is seen at Carlisle headed by BR Standard 'Britannia' Class 7MT 4-6-2 No. 70013 'Oliver Cromwell' (with painted name) after hauling train 1T57 from Manchester Victoria via the Settle & Carlisle line. This once-in-a-lifetime trip began and ended in Liverpool and was hauled at various stages by four different steam locos. No. 70013 has since been preserved and has now returned to main line running.

NOVEMBER

5
Monday

6
Tuesday

7
Wednesday

8
Thursday

9
Friday

10
Saturday

Remembrance Day

11
Sunday

NOVEMBER

M	T	W	T	F	S	S
			1	2	3	4
5	6	7	8	9	10	11
12	13	14	15	16	17	18
19	20	21	22	23	24	25
26	27	28	29	30		

York depot in the 1960s — on the left is Peppercorn Class 'A1' 4-6-2 No. 60121 'Silurian' while in the foreground ex-LNER 'V2' 2-6-2 No. 60876 obscures the identity of the BR Standard Class 9F 2-10-0 behind. Both locos were then allocated to York and were withdrawn in October 1965. The SR 'Merchant Navy' 4-6-2 seen on the right has strayed far from its home territory.

NOVEMBER

12
Monday

13
Tuesday

14
Wednesday

15
Thursday

16
Friday

17
Saturday

18
Sunday

NOVEMBER

M	T	W	T	F	S	S
			1	2	3	4
5	6	7	8	9	10	11
12	13	14	15	16	17	18
19	20	21	22	23	24	25
26	27	28	29	30		

One of the many non-standard classes of locomotives that British Railways inherited were these ancient LSWR's Drummond Class 'T9' 4-4-0s. Here No. 30120, built in 1899 and the only member of this class to be preserved, spends its last days on light passenger duties in North Cornwall. It is seen leaving Wadebridge station with a train for Exeter in the late 1950s.

NOVEMBER

19
Monday

20
Tuesday

21
Wednesday

22
Thursday

23
Friday

24
Saturday

25
Sunday

	NOVEMBER					
M	T	W	T	F	S	S
			1	2	3	4
5	6	7	8	9	10	11
12	13	14	15	16	17	18
19	20	21	22	23	24	25
26	27	28	29	30		

The end is nigh — BR Standard Class 4MT 2-6-0 No. 76088 simmers in the early spring sunshine at Croes Newydd depot, Wrexham, on 13 March 1967. Apart from the narrow gauge Vale of Rheidol Railway, BR steam was soon to be eradicated from Wales — Croes Newydd depot closed on 5 June. No. 76088 had a very short life — it was delivered new in May 1957 and was withdrawn on 30 June 1967.

NOVEMBER/DECEMBER

26
Monday

27
Tuesday

28
Wednesday

29
Thursday

30
Friday

1
Saturday

2
Sunday

			NOVEMBER			
M	T	W	T	F	S	S
			1	2	3	4
5	6	7	8	9	10	11
12	13	14	15	16	17	18
19	20	21	22	23	24	25
26	27	28	29	30		

Ex-LNER Class 'Q6' 0-8-0 No. 63406 lays a good layer of soot over Baldon Colliery station as it charges through with coal from Seaham for the Tyneside power stations. Introduced by the North Eastern Railway in 1913 the 'Q6' class remained more-or-less intact until the 1960s with the last members being withdrawn as late as 1967.

DECEMBER

3
Monday

4
Tuesday

5
Wednesday

6
Thursday

7
Friday

8
Saturday

9
Sunday

DECEMBER						
M	T	W	T	F	S	S
					1	2
3	4	5	6	7	8	9
10	11	12	13	14	15	16
17	18	19	20	21	22	23
24	25	26	27	28	29	30
31						

Ex-North British Railway Class 'J37' 0-6-0 No. 64611 catches the evening sun at it hustles a north-bound trip freight through Dunfermline Lower station on 14 September 1966. The 'J37s' were introduced in 1914 and many survived until the end of steam in Scotland — No. 64611 was withdrawn from Dundee Tay Bridge depot in April 1967.

DECEMBER

10
Monday

11
Tuesday

12
Wednesday

13
Thursday

14
Friday

15
Saturday

16
Sunday

DECEMBER						
M	T	W	T	F	S	S
					1	2
3	4	5	6	7	8	9
10	11	12	13	14	15	16
17	18	19	20	21	22	23
24	25	26	27	28	29	30
31						

Then allocated to Plymouth Laira depot, ex-GWR '4575' Class 2-6-2T No. 5569 pulls out of Tavistock South station with two auto trailers shortly before closure of the ex-GW line to Launceston at the end of 1962. The loco was built at Swindon in 1929 and withdrawn from Southall depot at the end of 1964.

DECEMBER

17
Monday

18
Tuesday

19
Wednesday

20
Thursday

21
Friday

22
Saturday

23
Sunday

DECEMBER						
M	T	W	T	F	S	S
					1	2
3	4	5	6	7	8	9
10	11	12	13	14	15	16
17	18	19	20	21	22	23
24	25	26	27	28	29	30
31						

Allocated to Cricklewood depot, ex-LMS 'Crab' 2-6-0 No. 42774 waits to depart from St Pancras station with a boat train of smart 'blood and custard' coaches for Tilbury on 11 July 1953. Built at Crewe in 1927, the 'Crab' was withdrawn from Manningham shed in November 1963.

DECEMBER

24
Monday

Christmas Day

25
Tuesday

Boxing Day

26
Wednesday

27
Thursday

28
Friday

29
Saturday

30
Sunday

DECEMBER						
M	T	W	T	F	S	S
					1	2
3	4	5	6	7	8	9
10	11	12	13	14	15	16
17	18	19	20	21	22	23
24	25	26	27	28	29	30
31						

Ex-Caledonian railway McIntosh-designed Class 2P 0-4-4T No. 55164 lets off steam at Moffat
station, the terminus of the short branch line from Beattock, while on the daily freight turn on 10 July
1958. Built at St Rollox in 1900 the loco was withdrawn from Beattock depot in February 1959.
The Moffat branch lost its passenger service on 6 December 1954 and closed completely on 6 April
1964.

DECEMBER /JANUARY

31
Monday

New Year's Day

1
Tuesday

2
Wednesday

3
Thursday

4
Friday

5
Saturday

6
Sunday

			JANUARY			
M	T	W	T	F	S	S
	1	2	3	4	5	6
7	8	9	10	11	12	13
14	15	16	17	18	19	20
21	22	23	24	25	26	27
28	29	30	31			

	JANUARY	FEBRUARY	MARCH	APRIL	MAY	JUNE
M						
T					1	
W		1			2	
T		2	1		3	
F		3	2		4	1
S		4	3		5	2
S	1	5	4	1	6	3
M	2	6	5	2	7	4
T	3	7	6	3	8	5
W	4	8	7	4	9	6
T	5	9	8	5	10	7
F	6	10	9	6	11	8
S	7	11	10	7	12	9
S	8	12	11	8	13	10
M	9	13	12	9	14	11
T	10	14	13	10	15	12
W	11	15	14	11	16	13
T	12	16	15	12	17	14
F	13	17	16	13	18	15
S	14	18	17	14	19	16
S	15	19	18	15	20	17
M	16	20	19	16	21	18
T	17	21	20	17	22	19
W	18	22	21	18	23	20
T	19	23	22	19	24	21
F	20	24	23	20	25	22
S	21	25	24	21	26	23
S	22	26	25	22	27	24
M	23	27	26	23	28	25
T	24	28	27	24	29	26
W	25	29	28	25	30	27
T	26		29	26	31	28
F	27		30	27		29
S	28		31	28		30
S	29			29		
M	30			30		
T	31					

2012 PLANNER

	JULY	AUGUST	SEPTEMBER	OCTOBER	NOVEMBER	DECEMBER
M				1		
T				2		
W		1		3		
T		2		4	1	
F		3		5	2	
S		4	1	6	3	1
S	1	5	2	7	4	2
M	2	6	3	8	5	3
T	3	7	4	9	6	4
W	4	8	5	10	7	5
T	5	9	6	11	8	6
F	6	10	7	12	9	7
S	7	11	8	13	10	8
S	8	12	9	14	11	9
M	9	13	10	15	12	10
T	10	14	11	16	13	11
W	11	15	12	17	14	12
T	12	16	13	18	15	13
F	13	17	14	19	16	14
S	14	18	15	20	17	15
S	15	19	16	21	18	16
M	16	20	17	22	19	17
T	17	21	18	23	20	18
W	18	22	19	24	21	19
T	19	23	20	25	22	20
F	20	24	21	26	23	21
S	21	25	22	27	24	22
S	22	26	23	28	25	23
M	23	27	24	29	26	24
T	24	28	25	30	27	25
W	25	29	26	31	28	26
T	26	30	27		29	27
F	27	31	28		30	28
S	28		29			29
S	29		30			30
M	30					31
T	31					

	JANUARY	FEBRUARY	MARCH	APRIL	MAY	JUNE
M				1		
T	1			2		
W	2			3	1	
T	3			4	2	
F	4	1	1	5	3	
S	5	2	2	6	4	1
S	6	3	3	7	5	2
M	7	4	4	8	6	3
T	8	5	5	9	7	4
W	9	6	6	10	8	5
T	10	7	7	11	9	6
F	11	8	8	12	10	7
S	12	9	9	13	11	8
S	13	10	10	14	12	9
M	14	11	11	15	13	10
T	15	12	12	16	14	11
W	16	13	13	17	15	12
T	17	14	14	18	16	13
F	18	15	15	19	17	14
S	19	16	16	20	18	15
S	20	17	17	21	19	16
M	21	18	18	22	20	17
T	22	19	19	23	21	18
W	23	20	20	24	22	19
T	24	21	21	25	23	20
F	25	22	22	26	24	21
S	26	23	23	27	25	22
S	27	24	24	28	26	23
M	28	25	25	29	27	24
T	29	26	26	30	28	25
W	30	27	27		29	26
T	31	28	28		30	27
F			29		31	28
S			30			29
S			31			30
M						
T						

2013 PLANNER

	JULY	AUGUST	SEPTEMBER	OCTOBER	NOVEMBER	DECEMBER
M	1					
T	2			1		
W	3			2		
T	4	1		3		
F	5	2		4	1	
S	6	3		5	2	
S	7	4	1	6	3	1
M	8	5	2	7	4	2
T	9	6	3	8	5	3
W	10	7	4	9	6	4
T	11	8	5	10	7	5
F	12	9	6	11	8	6
S	13	10	7	12	9	7
S	14	11	8	13	10	8
M	15	12	9	14	11	9
T	16	13	10	15	12	10
W	17	14	11	16	13	11
T	18	15	12	17	14	12
F	19	16	13	18	15	13
S	20	17	14	19	16	14
S	21	18	15	20	17	15
M	22	19	16	21	18	16
T	23	20	17	22	19	17
W	24	21	18	23	20	18
T	25	22	19	24	21	19
F	26	23	20	25	22	20
S	27	24	21	26	23	21
S	28	25	22	27	24	22
M	29	26	23	28	25	23
T	30	27	24	29	26	24
W	31	28	25	30	27	25
T		29	26	31	28	26
F		30	27		29	27
S		31	28		30	28
S			29			29
M			30			30
T						31

2013

JANUARY
```
M  T  W  T  F  S  S
      1  2  3  4  5  6
 7  8  9 10 11 12 13
14 15 16 17 18 19 20
21 22 23 24 25 26 27
28 29 30 31
```

FEBRUARY
```
M  T  W  T  F  S  S
            1  2  3
 4  5  6  7  8  9 10
11 12 13 14 15 16 17
18 19 20 21 22 23 24
25 26 27 28
```

MARCH
```
M  T  W  T  F  S  S
            1  2  3
 4  5  6  7  8  9 10
11 12 13 14 15 16 17
18 19 20 21 22 23 24
25 26 27 28 29 30 31
```

APRIL
```
M  T  W  T  F  S  S
 1  2  3  4  5  6  7
 8  9 10 11 12 13 14
15 16 17 18 19 20 21
22 23 24 25 26 27 28
29 30
```

MAY
```
M  T  W  T  F  S  S
      1  2  3  4  5
 6  7  8  9 10 11 12
13 14 15 16 17 18 19
20 21 22 23 24 25 26
27 28 29 30 31
```

JUNE
```
M  T  W  T  F  S  S
               1  2
 3  4  5  6  7  8  9
10 11 12 13 14 15 16
17 18 19 20 21 22 23
24 25 26 27 28 29 30
```

JULY
```
M  T  W  T  F  S  S
 1  2  3  4  5  6  7
 8  9 10 11 12 13 14
15 16 17 18 19 20 21
22 23 24 25 26 27 28
29 30 31
```

AUGUST
```
M  T  W  T  F  S  S
         1  2  3  4
 5  6  7  8  9 10 11
12 13 14 15 16 17 18
19 20 21 22 23 24 25
26 27 28 29 30 31
```

SEPTEMBER
```
M  T  W  T  F  S  S
                  1
 2  3  4  5  6  7  8
 9 10 11 12 13 14 15
16 17 18 19 20 21 22
23 24 25 26 27 28 29
30
```

OCTOBER
```
M  T  W  T  F  S  S
   1  2  3  4  5  6
 7  8  9 10 11 12 13
14 15 16 17 18 19 20
21 22 23 24 25 26 27
28 29 30 31
```

NOVEMBER
```
M  T  W  T  F  S  S
         1  2  3
 4  5  6  7  8  9 10
11 12 13 14 15 16 17
18 19 20 21 22 23 24
25 26 27 28 29 30
```

DECEMBER
```
M  T  W  T  F  S  S
                  1
 2  3  4  5  6  7  8
 9 10 11 12 13 14 15
16 17 18 19 20 21 22
23 24 25 26 27 28 29
30 31
```

2014

JANUARY
```
M  T  W  T  F  S  S
      1  2  3  4  5
 6  7  8  9 10 11 12
13 14 15 16 17 18 19
20 21 22 23 24 25 26
27 28 29 30 31
```

FEBRUARY
```
M  T  W  T  F  S  S
               1  2
 3  4  5  6  7  8  9
10 11 12 13 14 15 16
17 18 19 20 21 22 23
24 25 26 27 28
```

MARCH
```
M  T  W  T  F  S  S
               1  2
 3  4  5  6  7  8  9
10 11 12 13 14 15 16
17 18 19 20 21 22 23
24 25 26 27 28 29 30
31
```

APRIL
```
M  T  W  T  F  S  S
   1  2  3  4  5  6
 7  8  9 10 11 12 13
14 15 16 17 18 19 20
21 22 23 24 25 26 27
28 29 30
```

MAY
```
M  T  W  T  F  S  S
      1  2  3  4
 5  6  7  8  9 10 11
12 13 14 15 16 17 18
19 20 21 22 23 24 25
26 27 28 29 30 31
```

JUNE
```
M  T  W  T  F  S  S
                  1
 2  3  4  5  6  7  8
 9 10 11 12 13 14 15
16 17 18 19 20 21 22
23 24 25 26 27 28 29
30
```

JULY
```
M  T  W  T  F  S  S
   1  2  3  4  5  6
 7  8  9 10 11 12 13
14 15 16 17 18 19 20
21 22 23 24 25 26 27
28 29 30 31
```

AUGUST
```
M  T  W  T  F  S  S
            1  2  3
 4  5  6  7  8  9 10
11 12 13 14 15 16 17
18 19 20 21 22 23 24
25 26 27 28 29 30 31
```

SEPTEMBER
```
M  T  W  T  F  S  S
 1  2  3  4  5  6  7
 8  9 10 11 12 13 14
15 16 17 18 19 20 21
22 23 24 25 26 27 28
29 30
```

OCTOBER
```
M  T  W  T  F  S  S
      1  2  3  4  5
 6  7  8  9 10 11 12
13 14 15 16 17 18 19
20 21 22 23 24 25 26
27 28 29 30 31
```

NOVEMBER
```
M  T  W  T  F  S  S
               1  2
 3  4  5  6  7  8  9
10 11 12 13 14 15 16
17 18 19 20 21 22 23
24 25 26 27 28 29 30
```

DECEMBER
```
M  T  W  T  F  S  S
 1  2  3  4  5  6  7
 8  9 10 11 12 13 14
15 16 17 18 19 20 21
22 23 24 25 26 27 28
29 30 31
```

2015

JANUARY
```
M  T  W  T  F  S  S
         1  2  3  4
 5  6  7  8  9 10 11
12 13 14 15 16 17 18
19 20 21 22 23 24 25
26 27 28 29 30 31
```

FEBRUARY
```
M  T  W  T  F  S  S
                  1
 2  3  4  5  6  7  8
 9 10 11 12 13 14 15
16 17 18 19 20 21 22
23 24 25 26 27 28
```

MARCH
```
M  T  W  T  F  S  S
                  1
 2  3  4  5  6  7  8
 9 10 11 12 13 14 15
16 17 18 19 20 21 22
23 24 25 26 27 28 29
30 31
```

APRIL
```
M  T  W  T  F  S  S
      1  2  3  4  5
 6  7  8  9 10 11 12
13 14 15 16 17 18 19
20 21 22 23 24 25 26
27 28 29 30
```

MAY
```
M  T  W  T  F  S  S
         1  2  3
 4  5  6  7  8  9 10
11 12 13 14 15 16 17
18 19 20 21 22 23 24
25 26 27 28 29 30 31
```

JUNE
```
M  T  W  T  F  S  S
 1  2  3  4  5  6  7
 8  9 10 11 12 13 14
15 16 17 18 19 20 21
22 23 24 25 26 27 28
29 30
```

JULY
```
M  T  W  T  F  S  S
      1  2  3  4  5
 6  7  8  9 10 11 12
13 14 15 16 17 18 19
20 21 22 23 24 25 26
27 28 29 30 31
```

AUGUST
```
M  T  W  T  F  S  S
               1  2
 3  4  5  6  7  8  9
10 11 12 13 14 15 16
17 18 19 20 21 22 23
24 25 26 27 28 29 30
31
```

SEPTEMBER
```
M  T  W  T  F  S  S
   1  2  3  4  5  6
 7  8  9 10 11 12 13
14 15 16 17 18 19 20
21 22 23 24 25 26 27
28 29 30
```

OCTOBER
```
M  T  W  T  F  S  S
         1  2  3  4
 5  6  7  8  9 10 11
12 13 14 15 16 17 18
19 20 21 22 23 24 25
26 27 28 29 30 31
```

NOVEMBER
```
M  T  W  T  F  S  S
                  1
 2  3  4  5  6  7  8
 9 10 11 12 13 14 15
16 17 18 19 20 21 22
23 24 25 26 27 28 29
30
```

DECEMBER
```
M  T  W  T  F  S  S
   1  2  3  4  5  6
 7  8  9 10 11 12 13
14 15 16 17 18 19 20
21 22 23 24 25 26 27
28 29 30 31
```

THREE YEAR PLANNER

2013

2014

2015

ADDRESSES

Name:

Address:

Telephone:

Email:

Name:

Address:

Telephone:

Email:

Name:

Address:

Telephone:

Email:

Name:

Address:

Telephone:

Email:

Name:

Address:

Telephone:

Email:

Name:

Address:

Telephone:

Email:

Name:

Address:

Telephone:

Email:

Name:

Address:

Telephone:

Email:

Name:

Address:

Telephone:

Email:

Name:

Address:

Telephone:

Email:

Name:

Address:

Telephone:

Email:

Name:

Address:

Telephone:

Email:

Name:

Address:

Telephone:

Email:

Name:

Address:

Telephone:

Email:

Name:

Address:

Telephone:

Email:

Name:

Address:

Telephone:

Email:

Name:

Address:

Telephone:

Email:

Name:

Address:

Telephone:

Email:

Name:

Address:

Telephone:

Email:

Name:

Address:

Telephone:

Email:

Name:

Address:

Telephone:

Email:

Name:

Address:

Telephone:

Email:

Name: _____

Address: _____

_____

_____

Telephone: _____

Email: _____

Name: _____

Address: _____

_____

_____

Telephone: _____

Email: _____

Name: _____

Address: _____

_____

_____

Telephone: _____

Email: _____

Name: _____

Address: _____

_____

_____

Telephone: _____

Email: _____

Name: _____

Address: _____

_____

_____

Telephone: _____

Email: _____

Name: _____

Address: _____

_____

_____

Telephone: _____

Email: _____

Name: _____

Address: _____

_____

_____

Telephone: _____

Email: _____

Name: _____

Address: _____

_____

_____

Telephone: _____

Email: _____

NOTES

LOVED THIS BOOK?

Tell us what you think and you could win another fantastic
book from David & Charles in our monthly prize draw.
www.lovethisbook.co.uk

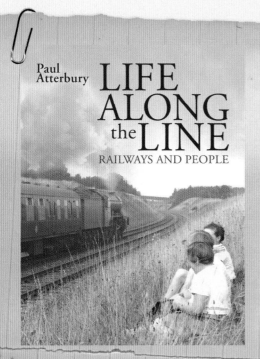

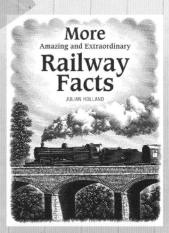

LIFE ALONG THE LINE
Paul Atterbury
ISBN 978-0-7153-3628-1
Life Along the Line takes a nostalgic look at the
world of British railways through the eyes of best-
selling author and antiques expert Paul Atterbury.

**MORE AMAZING AND EXTRAORDINARY RAIL-
WAY FACTS**
Julian Holland
ISBN 978-0-7153-3622-9
The second fascinating miscellany that will delight
railway buffs everywhere. From the famous
steam trains of the Great Western Railway and
celebrated British locomotive builders to Victorian
navvies and the 'second' Beeching Report.

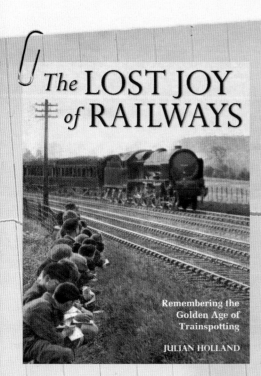

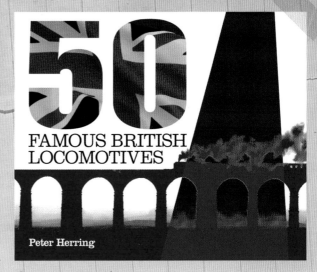

THE LOST JOY OF RAILWAYS
Julian Holland
ISBN 978-0-7153-3847-6
A book to transport you back to the 1950s and
60s, reminding you not just of the trains but of
personal accounts, journey logs, timetables and
photographs.

FIFTY FAMOUS BRITISH LOCOMOTIVES
Peter Herring
ISBN 978-0-7153-3343-3
A nostalgic guide to fifty of the most famous
locomotives of the steam train and early diesel
age, including the people, power and popularity
that made them famous.

David & Charles publish high quality books on a wide range of subjects.
For more great book ideas visit www.rubooks.co.uk

A DAVID & CHARLES BOOK
© F&W Media International LTD 2011

David & Charles is an imprint of F&W Media International, LTD
Brunel House, Forde Close, Newton Abbot, TQ12 4PU, UK

F&W Media International, LTD is a subsidiary of F+W Media, Inc., 4700 East
Galbraith Road
Cincinnati OH45236, USA

First published in the UK in 2011

Text copyright © Julian Holland 2011
Image copyright © see below

Julian Holland has asserted his right to be identified as author of this work in
accordance with the Copyright, Designs and Patents Act, 1988.

All rights reserved. No part of this publication may be reproduced, stored in
a retrieval system, or transmitted, in any form or by any means, electronic or
mechanical, by photocopying, recording or otherwise, without prior permission
in writing from the publisher.

The publisher has endeavoured to contact all contributors of images for permission to reproduce. If there are any errors or omissions please send notice in
writing to David & Charles Ltd, who will be happy to make any amendments in
subsequent printings.

A catalogue record for this book is available from the British Library.

ISBN-13: 978-1-4463-0122-7
ISBN-10: 1-4463-0122-2

Printed in China Toppan Leefung Printing Limited for:
F&W Media International, LTD
Brunel House, Forde Close, Newton Abbot, TQ12 4PU, UK

Commissioning Editor: Neil Baber
Editor: Verity Muir
Design Manager: Sarah Clark
Production Controller: Kelly Smith

F+W Media publishes high quality books on a wide range of subjects
For more great book ideas visit: www.rubooks.co.uk

PICTURE CREDITS

Pages 2–3 (clockwise from top left) *70010 Norwich* **M C Kemp**; *62011 Alnwick* **I S Carr**; *30933 Tunbridge Wells* **I S Carr**; *32331 London Bridge* **I S Carr**; *42081 Redhill* **Stanley Creer**; Pages 4 *(5042 MerchantVenturer)* **No credit;** Week1 *(45650 Manchester Victoria)* **Jim Carter**; Week 2 *(6874 Plymouth)*, Week 5 *(7005 Maidenhead)*, Week 7 *(60010 Gas Works Tunnel)*, Week 8 *(60124 Belle Isle)*, Week 12 *(46115 Carstairs)*, Week 30 *(1006 Saltash)*, Week 31 *(34079 Plymouth)*, **Gerald T Robinson**; Week 3 *(70016 Teignmouth)* **R W Hinton**; Week 4 *(7015 Hemerdon)* **T E Williams**; Week 6 *(1027 Box)*, Week 29 *(6999 Bruton)* **G A Richardson**; Week 9 *(60154 York)*, Week 40 *(60124 Eaglescliffe)*, Week 45 *(70013 Carlisle)* **I S Carr**; Week 10 *(60092 Newcastle)*, Week 11 *(60034 Newcastle)*, Week 35 *(60022 King's Cross)*, Week 49 *(63406 Boldon Colliery)* **M Dunnett**; Week 13 *(6952 Basingstoke)*, Week 14 *(4610 Exeter St Davids)*, Week 15 *(45565 Glos Eastgate)*, Week 16 *(7005 Cheltenham Lansdown)*, Week 17 *(75061 Glos Barnwood)*, Week 20 *(34071 Salisbury)*, Week 22 *(60024 Glasgow)* **Julian Holland;** Week 19 *(Newton Abbot depot)*, Week 36 *(35013 Salisbury)* **D H Ballantyne**; Week 21 *(60109 Leeds)*, Week 23 *(45501 Stockport)*, Week 25 *(45524 Linthwaite)*, Week 38 *(34013 Brighton)*, Week 41 *(62739 Scarborough)* **Kenneth Field**; Week 24 *(70022 Shap)* **M C Kemp**; Week 26 *(46140 Carlisle)* **John S Whiteley**; Week 28 *(4507 Taunton)*, Week 37 *(Bristolian)* **J R Smith**; Week 32 *(45503 Hartford)* **N F W Dyckhoff**; Week 33 *(46225 Shap)*, Week 34 *(60035 Edinburgh Haymarket)*, Week 47 *(30120 Wadebridge)*, Week 1 (2013) *(55164 Moffat)* **D A Anderson**; Week 39 *(30829 Exeter Central)*, Week 46 *(60876 York)* **John K Morton**; Week 42 *(46118 Crewe)* **R F Roberts**; Week 43 *(60014 Edinburgh)* **W S Sellar**; Week 44 *(70052 Crewe South)* **Mike Turner**; Week 48 *(76088 Wrexham)* **R Siviter**; Week 50 *(64611 Dunfermline)* **Rev Graham B Wise**; Week 51 *(5569 Tavistock)* **Peter Bowles**; Week 52 *(42774 St Pancras)* **Stanley Creer**; Week 27 *(45517 Shap)* **No credit**.